THANK YOU
FOR YOUR SERVICE

*The Trials and Triumphs from the Journey of a
Female Army Sergeant in Desert Storm*

By Tonya "TanktheNurse" Kerrin

10-10-10
Publishing

THANK YOU FOR YOUR SERVICE: The Trials and Triumphs from the Journey of a Female Army Sergeant in Desert Storm
www.thankyouforyourservicebook.com
Copyright © 2023 Tonya Kerrin

Paperback ISBN: 979-8-376056-62-2

References to internet websites (URLs) were accurate at the time of writing. Authors and the publishers are not responsible for URLs that may have expired or changed since the manuscript was prepared.

Limits of Liability and Disclaimer of Warranty
The author and publisher shall not be liable for your misuse of the enclosed material. This book is strictly for informational and educational purposes only.

Medical Disclaimer
The medical or health information in this book is provided as an information resource only and is not to be used or relied on for any diagnostic or treatment purposes. This information is not intended to be patient education, does not create any patient-physician relationship, and should not be used as a substitute for professional diagnosis and treatment.
Warning – Disclaimer
The purpose of this book is to educate and entertain. The author and/or publisher do not guarantee that anyone following these techniques, suggestions, tips, ideas, or strategies will become successful. The author and/or publisher shall have neither liability nor responsibility to anyone with respect to any loss or damage caused, or alleged to be caused, directly or indirectly by the information contained in this book.

Publisher
10-10-10 Publishing
Markham, ON Canada

Printed in Canada and the United States of America

*This book is dedicated to all the men and women
who currently serve or have served in any branch of the military,
along with the families of the service person.*

*My family: Charlotte Swayne (my mother), Toni Howard,
Tracy Bloom and Anton Kerrin (my siblings); Rashad Fields,
Ahmaad Fields, Isaiah Fields (my sons); Ramir Fields, Aiyanna Fields,
Shani Fields, Tianna Fields, Nahmya Fields, Kaylani Fields,
Amyra Fields, Ahdaia Fields, Juliana Fields and Naomi Jeffries
(my 10 Cocos grandchildren); David Brown, Tina Moody,
Vontel Brown, Anthony Brown, Demetrius Brown, Thomas Brown,
Tina (Williams) Brown, James Williams and Andre (Sput) Williams
(close cousins); Aunt Barbara Ruth Brown, Aunt Teresa Williams,
Uncle Anton and Aunt Dee, Aunt Renee Blow and Uncle Sam Blow.*

*And, of course, I dedicate this book to CSM Nathaniel Wilson and
Sergeant Major Eloise Wilson, Dominic Gulley, Tony Thomas, Kenny
Jacobs, Robert Small, Doug Carter, Robert and Margie Kalaluhi,Ocea
Smith, Amy Fox-Sims, Donna Digan, Phillip Gulley and soldiers I
served with in Desert Storm, of 326th Med Battalion (Air Assault)
and 501st FSB Friedberg Germany.*

TABLE OF CONTENTS

Acknowledgements

I would first like to thank my family for supporting me and being there for me throughout this journey. First, Charlotte Swayne, my mom, raising her four kids as a single mother. She was an example to me throughout my life. Aunt Barbara Ruth Brown and Aunt Teresa for also being examples of how to be a mother, lady and strong woman. Toni Howard, Tracy Bloom and Anton Kerrin, my siblings, who also supported me as I chose every endeavor. In loving memory of everything you put in me, Mary M. Miller, my grandmother, and Sheridan Kerrin, my father.

I would like to thank my sons, Rashad Fields, Ahmaad Fields and Isaiah Fields, along with Serena Fields, Nina Fields and my 10 wonderful Cocos (grandchildren), Ramir, Aiyanna, Shani, Tianna, Nahmya, Kaylani, Amyra, Ahdaiah, Juliana and Naomi. I would not be who I am without all your love and support at all times. My sons learned to love and understand a strong militant mother, helping while I went to nursing school late in life, from carrying my book bag to helping me study, to staying out of the way while I accomplished the goals. My grandchildren for loving me and teaching me how to retire from the military and change from inspecting everything (military inspection style) and, of course, giving me my name, "TanktheNurse."

For bonuses go to ...

Thank you, Maxine Frederick (Sister Dee), for being a loving sister, friend, mentor, major influencer and advisor in my life in all areas, and for helping me to be the person I am. I can't thank you enough, Amy Sims-Fox and Ocea Smith, for guiding me during my tour at Ft. Campbell, KY, and for always being there throughout life.

I am deeply appreciative for my great friend, my Ride-and-Die for Life, Sherry Berry, for your enormous example of love, family, caregiving, strength and more. Thank you for always being there and showing up in my life in amazing ways, from my school days to infinity. Thank you!

I am extremely grateful to one of the most amazing people in the world, Lula Negash, for her example of friendship and family, and for studying the Bible with me and helping me to become a baptized Jehovah Witness. Lula has supported me throughout my civilian journey, multiple jobs and adventures, and put up with me at my most militant times, to my gentle times, wellness and illness. Thank you to Habrom Berhane, Asena Berhane, Emnet Abraha, Asgedome Abraha, Ruta Abraha and her entire family.

I would like to acknowledge and thank all of my ladies of the Wellness Group for being amazing people and inspiring me every day. They encourage me to strive each and every day to be better in all areas of my life: Sandy Brown-Deramus, Pat Brown, Cheryl Nnadi, Alberta Rucker, Tanya McCalahan, Renelle Taylor, Wendy Carper, Florence Blount, Jaqueline Johnson, Cheryle Carter, Cassandra Williams, Tarwana Lindsey, Mona Towns, Dorothy Jackson and Tracy Wilson.

I deeply appreciate Ashley Williams for being someone who constantly challenges me and supports me. You are an example, and I am proud and honored to have you in my life. Thank you, Cassandra, for sharing your beautiful daughter with me and allowing me to join her wellness team.

To the Columbus VA, I want to thank the team of doctors that make it a great place for veterans. I did not have a great experience when I returned in 1995, but a lot of changes were made, and the care received at the VA is above and beyond—Dr. Shaikh, Dr. Clay, Dr. Weibel and Dr. Zhang.

There are several amazing people that have crossed my path and allowed me to be in their lives: Kim and Tom Tandanpolie and the Ultimate Home Health Staff, Tony and Jenn Lowery, S. Yolanda Robinson, Masahide and Chantal Masuda, Seedra Eichleberger, Rejeana Haynes, Silvia Townsend, Michelle Madosky, Alisa Klepser, Khari Enaharo, Skip Young, Kate Ozebek and Julia Dutan.

To the entities and establishments that were a huge part of my journey to wellness and helping to maintain my health: Rusty Bucket Main St, especially Christina Kelly, Portia's Café and Natural Market, Grant Hospital, HomeReach Homecare, Riverside Hospital, Rasin Rack, Bexley Market, Clintonville Natural Market, Flavor 91, Dr. Kanodia and staff, Radiant Living (Vickie Gibbs, Malea Dicot), Kim Gunner, United Home Health, Rebecca Robinson Brown, Mitchell Brown and Lisa Gatto.

For bonuses go to ...

My personal health team, Dr. Marc Varkette and Dr. Zhang Remington.

Thank you to my Biofeedback community: Karen Avalon, Ryan Williams, Michaela Gomez, Donna Digan, Margie and Robert Kallaluhi, Alex, Tina, PT, Pam K, Cheryl, Marilyn, Marie, Chantal, Nannette, Dr. Adina, Joyce, Dr. Beverly, Alan, Barbara, Jovanna, Ruth, and Bernie.

Next Level Training: 44444444444 Especially Coach Denise Jones

My family, I thank you for all your support: Tiffany, Dante, Michael, Anthony, Demetrius, Jalisa, India, Mariah, Anton, Terrance and Noah.

The Ten: David, Tina, Vontel, Anthony, Demetrius, Thomas, Tracy, Toni and Anton.

The entire Ingram Family: Love you so much and am so grateful to have you in my life.

Thank you, Linda Kalafatis, for being my Soul Sissy and an amazing coach, not only in softball but in life.

My sisters and brothers in the truth: Thank you so much for all the support: Jack Selvage, Dareth Ashby, Kelly and Ed White, Cailey Domingues, Tom and Vicky Wiley, Lexi and Danielle, the Owens, the Pittmans, Laureen Cox and Diane Watson, Jackie Stiger, Deena Stiger, Barbara Bridges, Carol Stiger-Carson, Ron and Carla Chapman, Greg and Emma Allen and Paulette Hancock and Woody and Minguel Ingram.

The Swayne family, thank you, thank you.

A special thanks to The Incredibles- Gary and Pat Davis along with the entire family, Colleen, John William, Addie, Bridget and Robert, Kevin and Sarah, and their Children. I have learned a lot from all of you.

I would like to say a special thanks to Sherrod Brown (state senator) and all the support he gives to the veterans in Ohio.

About the Author

Tonya L. Kerrin lives in Columbus, Ohio, USA.

She still serves people every day with her holistic approach to wellness, providing classes, webinars, wellness retreats and more. She is available for in-person presentations, one-on-one consultations, training events and wellness evaluations. For rates and availability, please contact Tonya directly at: thankyouforyourservicebook.com.

To order more books, search for "Thank You for Your Service," on Amazon.com.

Finally, if you have been inspired by this book, the best thing you could ever do is pass that on and please take note when you see a veteran. When you say, "Thank you for your service," think of the sacrifice they made.

Foreword

Have you thanked a veteran for their service? Have you ever considered what sacrifices the soldier made, or what those sacrifices felt like?

Thank You for Your Service gives an inside look at the life of Tonya Kerrin, a 19-year-old female Columbus Ohio native, who became a 101 Airborne Air Assault, Screaming Eagles Sergeant and Desert Storm Veteran.

This book will show you why the excellence taught to soldiers, in the form of even the smallest disciplines, catapulted Tonya to a lifetime of battles fought with an array of different weapons. It also provides insight into the hard times of single parenthood, raising three black men in America, and instilling in them a sense of purpose, faith, excellence, and service.

Tonya's attitude toward serving and helping others doesn't end with her soldiers in the war zone. It continues with every person she meets, and helps to find purpose, peace and healing. Tonya is currently a certified instructor at The Center of Aromatherapy Research and Education, a wellness nurse consultant, and a speaker with a passion for helping people to find their inner strength, beauty, and purpose.

She also does one-on-one coaching for people with PTSD, depression, and other mental health issues. Her approach to healing is holistic, and combines biofeedback and aromatherapy, along with her own unique techniques.

The story of Tonya's journey will challenge your thinking, open your eyes to different perspectives, and encourage you to serve others with whatever gifts or skills you possess. It will show you what a brave woman can accomplish when she sets her mind to it.

In Tonya's words, "We all must face some difficult battles in life. Strength comes from how we choose to fight these battles."

Raymond Aaron
New York Times **Bestselling Author**

Chapter 1

The Start

*"You don't have to be great to start,
but you have to start to be great."*
– Zig Ziglar

Why Join?

The summer of 1983 was when it all started. Those days, life was different. It wasn't as fast paced as it is now, and people weren't as rushed. I was just a young girl then, enjoying my life just as any other high schooler would. I had my friends, and we would just hang out and have fun.

I was raised in a single-parent household. My mother and her sister, Aunt Barbara Ruth, along with my paternal Aunt Teresa, had been the ones looking after us. Getting all of us children ready for school every day wasn't as efficient as it should have been in my senior year. I was the one often getting dropped off late for school. At one point, I almost didn't graduate because I was mostly late. My first-period class was English, a course needed for graduation, and I was warned that if I was late one more time, I would not be able to attend the class. However, I'm not complaining; single parenthood comes with many challenges that most people don't understand.

I stayed with Aunt Barbara Ruth when not in school and worked for Sister's Chicken and Biscuits. This was a restaurant near her house.

In summer, we would go to her house till school resumed. This was where I met Everett, my to-be husband. More on this later.

Our family, "the Ingram family," was a large one and is great even today. However, there was something about us back then that really never agreed with me. We fought a lot. There was a lot of arguing going on all the time. Be it any event, we Ingrams knew how to turn it into a full-blown, knock-down, dragged-out brawl. And I really never became okay with that. We fought at family reunions, weddings, funerals... you name it. That thing had never settled inside of me. So, you could say that I was looking for an escape.

At school, I was always a good student and got good grades. I loved school life; it was just so much fun. I was actively involved in athletics and always tried to be the best. Basketball, volleyball, track, and softball were some of the sports I was into. Being a Mifflin Cowpuncher meant a big deal at that time.

The "Sugar Hill Gang" had been and is still my fondest memory of high school. Our gang had been inseparable. Almost all of us lived in the Somerset area and went to Mifflin High School. The community bond was really strong back then, and we were all each other had. Even when we were very young, we were there for each other through everything. Dominic and Kenny signed up for the navy as the time came to move on. Tony and Doug joined the army, whereas Robert went to the marines. Services to the country were big back then, and I recall being really proud of them.

When the army recruiter came to our school, I first thought about joining the forces. The recruiter was very eloquent and made a good case for joining the army. I took him up because I could be a nurse in the army. In addition, I had always wanted to help people, and this seemed like a perfect opportunity to do that.

I always had this desire inside of me to help others. Then, when I was eight, I was hit by a car while crossing the street. I was rushed to the hospital, and it was there that I met a nurse who took care of me. She was not kind and caring; my grandmother had to talk to her about how she treated me. That experience really made an impact on me, and I knew that I wanted to be better than her. When the recruiter came, all of this was in my subconscious. It was only in my 50s that I truly realized that it was that incident that had made me want to become a nurse.

This wasn't the only opportunity for nursing that came my way. As a young child, I would work with my grandmother at the Rosemont School for Girls. She was a cook there, and I would help her out in the kitchen. I loved being around the nuns. They were so sweet and had a big influence on my life. Carol Johnson was the administrator while Beverly Redman was the supervisor for my mom and aunt. Both worked with the girls in the cottage.

Later, I was hired in place of my grandmother when she was sick, or for special events. The school offered to send me to a nursing school In return for coming back and working for them. But at the time, I was only 17 and still in high school. So, I didn't truly grasp what was being offered to me.

Between the two nursing options I had at that time, the words of that army recruiter stuck with me. "We do more by 9 a.m. than most people do all day," he said. And that really resonated with me. I was always someone who strived to be the best and do more. So that's how I made my decision.

All my friends were joining the services, and my sister had settled in New York after her marriage. It was time for me to move on too, so I took up the offer.

Getting Ready and Prepared

Now, joining the army wasn't something that you could just do on a whim. I had to be prepared for it, both mentally and physically. The recruiter had given me a list of things I needed to do to join, and I got right to it.

Those who had known me then wouldn't define me as skinny or fat but rather "thick." I wasn't obese at any time in my life, but I definitely wasn't skinny either. The army requires you to be at a certain weight and body fat percentage to join, so I had to shed some weight and tone my body to meet the standards.

So, I started working out a bit and eating right. The sugar had to be cut out, and water intake had to be increased. There were no drastic steps, just basics done right. And in a few months, I got my weight and body fat down to where they needed to be. The process wasn't easy, but the results were worth it.

I mentioned Everett earlier. I had met him at Sisters Chicken and Biscuits. We started enjoying each other's company. I had yet to tell him about my plans to join the army, because I wanted to ensure everything was set in stone first. But once I started getting ready, there was no turning back. I told Everett about my plans, and he took it surprisingly well. That was because he was in the process of joining the army. He was supposed to leave for basic training a few weeks after me.

The First Flight

With the decision made up and my body now ready, all that was left to do was to take the first flight. I didn't have a living memory of flying in my life before that. My father was deployed in Alaska as a member of the air force military police when I was born, so my first years of life were spent in Alaska. Despite my father being in the air force police, I don't remember much about that time.

Anyway, I was ready for my first flight. The motivation and excitement to fly to South Carolina for the first time in my life were at an all-time high. The adventure ahead was waiting for me, and I couldn't wait to start.

Chapter 2

Basic Training

"Human greatness does not lie in wealth or power, but in character and goodness. People are just people, and all people have faults and shortcomings, but all of us are born with a basic goodness."
— Anne Frank

South Carolina was an entirely different world than Somerset.

Going into Fort Jackson, we felt just like any other newbie. We were all in the same boat, wide-eyed and scared of the unknown. But we soon realized that this was not going to be a cakewalk. The day you come out of the receiving building, you are already a part of the team. You have to know how to work hard and be precise. There is no room for error in the military. You have to be perfect all the time, especially when it comes to your uniform. If your shoes aren't shined or your bed isn't made perfectly, you will hear about it.

Character Building

Basic training was all about building future soldiers' characters. The goal was to make us into strong, capable people who could withstand anything that was thrown at us. They wanted to break us down and then build us back up again.

Every human feels they have a limit to what they can do. The military wants to show you that there is no limit. It wants to push you further than you ever thought possible, both mentally and physically.

There were times when I thought I couldn't go on, but I had to. I had to find that extra strength within me that I never knew existed. Every time I pushed my limits, I realized I was capable of so much more than I ever thought.

Teamwork, camaraderie, precision and resolve are all qualities that the military instills in its soldiers. And it all starts with basic training.

The "getting things done before 9 a.m." saying from my recruiter proved to be one hundred percent true in the military. You are always up before the sun, running and doing PT (physical training). Then it is breakfast and off to start the day's tasks. Some days we would have classes; other days we would be out on the field practicing what we had learned in class.

For someone like me who wants to be in the midst of things, the quote sat perfectly. I loved being up and about early in the morning, getting things done. It made me feel like I was accomplishing something. That would change later in my life, but that is for later.

Sleep Is Overrated

In basic training, you quickly learn that sleep is a luxury. You are always tired and there is never enough time to rest. The days are long and filled with physical activity and drills. There is little time for anything else. It was at this point I realized that the notion of sleep is overrated. You learn to function on very little sleep. You power through the fatigue and push yourself to keep going. It's not easy, but you do it because you have to. You don't have a choice.

In the army, there's a thing called O dark 30. This is the time you have to be up and ready to go, usually around 4:30 a.m. I remember many mornings being dragged out of bed, half-asleep and barely able to function. But I would push through it because that is what was expected of me. In a nutshell, you have to be prepared for anything and everything. That's what the military does to you; it makes you into a well-oiled machine.

Precision

The military is all about precision. Everything has to be done a certain way, and there is no room for error. This is something that I struggled with at first. I am not a perfectionist by any means, and I like to do things my own way. But in the army, there is only one way to do things—the right way.

It took me some time to get used to this way of thinking, but eventually, I did. And once I did, I realized that it was actually quite liberating. There was no more second-guessing myself or doubting whether I was doing things the right way.

The way you march, the way you talk, the way you stand—it all has to be done with precision. There is no room for sloppiness in the military. If two military people approach each other and decide to walk together, you'll see them syncing their steps perfectly. It looks like a dance, but it's really just precision in action. You start to walk, talk and move like a soldier—everything becomes second nature.

The precision is so detailed that trash in trash cans is not tolerated, and every bed has to be made perfectly with no wrinkles in the sheets. The uniform has to be starched and ironed to perfection. Everything around you has to be in a specific place, 6 inches from the wall, 12 inches from the other person's bed, etc. There is a place for everything, and everything has its place.

You learn when to have your hat on and when to take it off. You learn to always stand at attention when someone of a higher rank enters the room. There is a protocol for everything, and you follow it without question. The salute, the way you address someone of a higher rank, it's all done with precision.

Work Ethic

The military instills a strong work ethic in its soldiers. The physical part was hard for me as a 19-year-old, but I powered through it. Getting in shape was by far the hardest thing I had to do in my life, but it was also the most rewarding. The sense of accomplishment I felt when I completed basic training was indescribable.

We used to do a lot of pushups. I particularly did more than anyone else in my group. Throughout my life, I've always worn a smile on my face. Every time the drill sergeant would pass by, he would just say, "I know you're smiling, so give me some more pushups." And I would just do it with a smile on my face. It didn't seem hard to me. I'm always someone looking for the silver lining, so even when things were tough, I would just try and find the positive in it.

These pushups served me well in the physical training, as a certain number of pushups, sit-ups and a 2-mile run within a specified time had to be completed. The timing for the run would depend on gender and age. For instance, for a 19-year-old like me at that time, the 2 miles had to be under 10 minutes. For someone in their forties, it would be 15 minutes.

Weapons training formed the next integral part of the training. This was to ensure that every soldier could handle and shoot any type of weapon. Taking apart the M16, then putting it back together again, grenade training and target practice—these were all part of the weapons training.

Once during grenade training, I didn't throw it far away enough and it landed closer to people. A lot of people could have been hurt, but thankfully, they weren't. That was a close call and it made me realize that even the smallest mistake could have huge consequences. A huge X was put on my helmet after that, and I had to redo the training. I was so embarrassed, but I knew that I had to just power through it. I can never forget that incident because it was such a wake-up call for me.

Our drill sergeant used to say, "Either you can be a rock or a sponge. When you pour water on a sponge, it expands and soaks up everything. When you pour water on a rock, it just rolls over it. You can't put two rocks together; they will just bounce off each other. You need a sponge to soak up everything."

This lesson remained with me for the rest of my time in the military. I realized that in order to be successful, you need to be like a sponge—open-minded, willing to learn and able to adapt.

My experience in the military was one that I will never forget. It taught me so much about myself, things that I never would have discovered otherwise. It was a truly transformational experience. And then I graduated from basic training. Looking back at it, I can only find one word to describe it: WOW!

Chapter 3

Overseas

"Wherever you go, go with all your heart."
– Confucius

After the basic training and the initial discipline that the army instilled in me were complete, now was the time for Advanced Individual Training. AIT, as we call it, is where we focus on the skills that we will need for our chosen career in the army. The MOS, or Military Occupational Specialty, is the basic job in the army that we train for. For me, it was combat medic, which led to my career as an army nurse.

AIT

AIT was an entirely different experience and was held at Fort Sam Houston in San Antonio, Texas. Fort Sam is also referred in our army circles as "Country Club Sam," because it is considered one of the best duty stations. Sunshine, warmer temperatures and no snow were the norm in Texas, and I enjoyed every minute of it. Most surprising of all were the flying cockroaches! I had never seen anything like it, and to this day have never seen anything like it again.

The training was tough, and I had to study hard, but I loved being a combat medic. So many new friends were made during AIT, and we all helped each other out. A medic in the army is equivalent to an EMT or a paramedic in the civilian world, and I felt like I was making a difference.

Acute care, primary care and emergency care were all covered in our training. I'll tell more about this in later chapters, but for now, just suffice it to say that I was very proud to be a combat medic.

Another thing I picked up there was drinking. I was never much of a drinker before, but after AIT, it became a regular part of my social life. We had an NCO club at the base. An NCO is an officer that has not yet been commissioned, so those who've not yet been designated as captains or above are NCOs. Add to this that under-21s were allowed to drink at the base; it made for some great parties!

Well, now that I was done with AIT, it was time to be stationed somewhere. And that's when I got my first big surprise. I was being sent to Worms, Germany! From Columbus to Germany was a big change, and I had no idea what to expect. Before that, I had a few weeks to go back home.

Marriage

At the same time that I was doing my basic training and AIT, Everett was going through his own training. He came in as a combat engineer. So, while I was at Fort Sam, he was finishing up his own training. Everett and I kept in touch as often as we could, but it wasn't easy. There were no cell phones or social media back then, so we had to rely on letters and the pay phone. We had to time everything just right so that we could actually talk to each other.

As they say, absence makes the heart grow fonder, and by the time Everett got his leave, we were both more in love than ever—at least what we thought was love. So back in Columbus, during my leave before going to Germany, Everett proposed and I said yes.

Now, I was not going to be another Ingram who would have her wedding tainted by the infighting of the family. As I mentioned earlier, my family had been a nuisance when it came to family events. This one time, the bride had her dress ruined. Even my grandmother ended up in a police car. Even after that, she went home, changed her clothes and came back to fight more. No, I was not going to put up with that nonsense; my wedding would go off without a hitch!

So, we decided to go to the Justice of the Peace and get married without all the hoopla. It was a beautiful ceremony, and I will never forget it. Afterward, Sherry, the head of our Sugarhill Gang, took the lead and hosted a reception that evening at her house. To this day, I could never thank her enough for what she did. This group of friends is like family to me, and I love them all dearly.

Time was so short to get everything done, and we barely had any time to plan the wedding. But in the end, it all worked out. The very next day, we had to say goodbye. Everett was being stationed in California and I was off to Germany. It was a tough goodbye, but we both knew that it wouldn't be forever. It turned out that we would meet again after one year, but that's a story for another chapter.

21

New Country

A 19-year-old arriving in a new country is always going to be a bit nervous. But I had no idea what I was about to experience. I'll not hide it; I am a chicken when it comes to new things. The previous knowledge I had of Germany came from a TV show called *The Twilight Zone*, which talked about castles, werewolves and vampires. So, as you can imagine, I was more than a little apprehensive about what I was going to find there.

As it turned out, my imagination had run wild, and Germany was nothing like what I had expected. The first thing that struck me was the landscape. The castles of Frankfurt, Heidelberg and Stuttgart were unlike anything I had ever seen. I was in awe of the architecture and the way that the country had been able to preserve its history. It was still a bit scary for a 19-year-old girl to be in a new country all by herself.

Anyway, the first day I got back, I was really hungry. I took a walk downtown, and there I found a familiar place: McDonald's—there's a McDonald's in Germany. A Big Mac would feel like home. So, I went in and ordered myself a meal. It turned out that it tasted nothing like the Big Macs back home. It was a bit of a culture shock.

They wouldn't serve ice in drinks either, because of the water quality. So here I was, with a glass of warm soda and a Big Mac that didn't taste like a Big Mac. I was so disappointed, I couldn't even describe it. I threw the whole meal in the trash and went to pay. I handed over my dollars from back home and got change back in

Deutsche marks. I didn't even know what those were. It felt like a weird banknote, something like paper money. The culture shock was in full effect, and I was teary-eyed on my way back.

As soon as I came back to my barracks, I started crying like a little baby. I was so homesick, and I missed everyone back home so much. It was such a big change for me, going from the States to Germany. And this was when I met one of the angels in my life, Catherine Hall. Cat, as I call her, was a chaplain's assistant, and she took me under her wing and took great care of me for a long time, even after Germany. You'll hear her name later in the book, but this is the beginning of our relationship. So, the first day ended with me bawling my eyes out and missing home. But I had to get used to this new place; it was going to be my home for some time now.

Worm

Worm was a very small base and there was a lot of learning. So, I went to my job and it was a clinic. However, this clinic was unlike others. It was basically what urgent care would look like now. Due to it being on a military base, we had soldiers coming in with sick calls. We'd do IVs, X-rays and even suturing at times. A lab and pharmacy were attached to our clinic, so it was a very well-rounded place.

So, anything that needed urgent attention, came to our clinic. Soon I took charge of the lab and, from there, ended up setting up and running the main clinic on base. This was a huge responsibility, and I was just 20 years old at the time. Managing hundreds of patients a day, doing inventory and maintaining the clinic was no small feat, but I loved every second of it. There was never a dull moment, and I was able to learn so much.

Now, always being the athletic and sports girl since forever, the military was the perfect place to be. There were always sports going on, from football to volleyball to track. You name it and we had it. There were perks to playing, like getting to travel and getting off work early. When going to other cities for championships, our seniors would wager against us. So, the practices and involvements were a big thing for everyone. While the standards weren't to the international level, we still would compare to college or semi-pro teams.

Before I share the Berlin tournament story, a part I'd like to share is that although the army didn't encourage smoking or drinking, it was pretty easy to do so. Since we were young, it was hard to resist peer pressure, and many of us gave in. So, drinking became a big thing for us. I used to have a fluid bottle in my room that would be full of Seagram's 7 or vodka.

Our seniors would say that if you find any reason to have a drink, a party or a get-together, you should do so. And we followed that to a T. That's all we would do. We used to get a ration card in the military, and it was good for one month. This card would allow four cartons of cigarettes a month and some alcohol. Almost everyone smoked and drank. Nothing was odd about it.

So, anyway, we went to Berlin for a championship. Being the team we were, we won and went out to have a good time. The problem was that we were having such a good time that we were all over the place. The Berlin Police observed and reprimanded us. They clearly stated that if we didn't sober up, we wouldn't be able to return to our base. And we were like, "No, no, no. We won't drink. We're sorry." So, we quickly sobered up. From then onwards, I learned to keep a level head and not go overboard while still enjoying myself.

The first year of experience as a medic in the army was a lot. From Worm's to managing a clinic to going to Berlin, I had learned so much and had so many experiences.

Motherhood

Everett and I were trying to get assigned to the same place as we were married now, but that didn't happen until the end of the first year. Everett was assigned to Darmstadt, Germany as a combat engineer. So, being away from each other for so long and then being united again, was the best feeling ever.

So, one month later, what would you expect to happen? I got pregnant with our first child, Rashad. At that time, I didn't have my family around me. It was just this great nurse. She was the wife of a service person, and she became like an auntie to me. She took very good care and helped guide me through my pregnancy. I was able to fly my mom over to be with me for the birth of our first son, Rashad Fields. Rashad had been two weeks overdue, which led to me having an emergency cesarean section.

Holding my first child was such a beautiful experience. It was at that moment that everything else in my life didn't matter. However, having childbirth in the military isn't the same as in the civilian world. In the civilian world, after you have a baby, you have people around you to help you. You have your mom, your sisters and your friends. They bring you food and they're there for emotional support. In the military, you don't have people that come and clean your room. You get up and clean it on your own.

Even the nurses were stout and strict. They made me get up and start walking just hours after giving birth. Making the bed, cleaning the room... it was all on me. I had to do everything. It was challenging, but it made me a stronger person. After 4 weeks, I was to report back to duty. This led me to find a babysitter that I could trust.

Our first babysitter was a Greek lady. I can say that the basics I know about childcare, I learned from her. She was an amazing woman who took care of Rashad like he was her own. And because of that, I was able to focus on my job and be the best army nurse that I could be.

Later, we had a Puerto Rican babysitter, who was also great. Letty was like family to us. She lived in the same building as us; she was always there for my children and gave me a different learning experience when it came to childcare. The neighbors did their best to help with the children as well.

Two years later, Ahmaad was born in Heidelberg too. Both happened to be emergency C-sections. Now, you'd expect motherhood to be given some relaxation in the military, right? But it's not. Remember the O dark Thirty runs I used to do before I had children? Yeah, I still had to do them, being up before 6 for PT. Now, with children, I had to be up much earlier—fixing the bottles, getting the diaper bag and myself ready, and reporting to the base before 6, be it rain, snow or sunshine. It is meant to keep us in good physical shape, but as a new mom, it was hard. In the military, you have to always be ready. You have to be prepared for anything and to be sent anywhere.

There was another fascinating thing I noticed in Germany. Whenever you walked or passed through an area where the Holocaust had taken place, you would see wreaths or flowers placed there in memory of those who had died. It was a very sobering experience, to be honest. You could feel the energy of all those people who had been here. It's an experience that I can't define in words, but it definitely left an impression on me.

Bad Tolz

Anyway, my dream had always been to be a nurse. However, I met some amazing physician assistants in the army, and I thought I wanted to be a physician assistant. Everett wasn't a fan of the idea or of me going to a school for it. I then got promoted to sergeant and enrolled in Bad Tolz, an NCO school.

An NCO school is where you learn to really fine-tune being a soldier. This is a school for people of all militaries. Now, some people might think that being a female in the military gives you certain benefits. It does not; rather, it gives you more challenges. There's no such thing as a female being given privileges by other women. No, we all go through the same challenges and difficulties. Most women prior to that period, 1984–85, were in nursing. So, we had to learn how to work with men and learn the ways of the army.

And how do you think women are trained in the army? The same way men are. No, there is no separate but equal here. You learn to do what the men do, and sometimes that includes doing things that you're not comfortable with. But you have to do them anyway because that's part of being in the army. At Bad Tolz, you had to march in snow, sleep outdoors in sleeping bags in the cold and get up early in the morning for PT. It doesn't matter if you're a man or woman; you have to do the same things.

The precision and the manner in which we had to do things was different. You had to train; you had to shine your boots to where they looked like glass and you had to wear your uniform. Your room had to be clean, and each coat and hanger had to be 1 inch apart in your closet, with no dust anywhere. Everything had to be measured to precision every day. And then, within less than 24 hours, your room should appear as if you had done nothing—no water drops in the sink, no smears on the window or on the mirror.

Precision is key in the army. You learn how to be precise in your actions and your words because, in the army, lives depend on it.

Chapter 4

For Campbell

"Eagles come in all shapes and sizes, but you will recognize them chiefly by their attitudes."

— E. F. Schumacher

The next journey of my life took me to Fort Campbell, Kentucky. There are a handful of bases that are as interesting as this one. The geographic area is divided between two states and four cities. It's only addressed in Kentucky because of the post office. The main gate is in Tennessee and about a mile from the Kentucky border. There are two roads that come onto the base, one from Hopkinsville, Kentucky, and the other from Clarksville, Tennessee. If I could describe the vibe of the place, I would say this is the base that teaches you how to be a soldier.

Screaming Eagle

When I got to Fort Campbell, I quickly knew it was time. The Screaming Eagle patch was enough to let you know that this was no ordinary place. For me, it was an honor to become a Screaming Eagle. The significance of this patch is not just that it is the 101st Airborne Division; it is a history and a way of life. The 101st Airborne has been in some of the most historic battles, from D-Day to Normandy to Bastogne, and even more recently in Afghanistan.

The way the patch works is that before you go to war, you wear your patch, which defines what unit you're with and what base you're on. If you go to war with that unit, then you are then authorized to put a patch on the other shoulder. So, I had double Screaming Eagles, which is no less than amazing.

Perfection

My superior was a very sharp man that went by the name of Sergeant Major Wilson (CSM, which stands for Command Sergeant Major). If you ever want to witness the epitome of a soldier, then you need to meet CSM Wilson. He was the kind of man that led by example. For me, his blood was a camouflage, to say the least.

Everett was stationed as a combat engineer on the far opposite side of the base, which would be the Kentucky side, whereas I was in the 326 Medical Battalion on the Tennessee side. From working in a clinic during my stay in Germany, to becoming an ambulance driver at Fort Campbell, my roles and responsibilities increased manyfold. Back there, it was labs and suturing and shifting patients we couldn't manage, to Heidelberg or Mannheim. Now it was working at the motor pool, driving Humvees and military ambulances while still doing the PT every single day. The march, the cadence, the songs... they all sound so vivid in my head even now.

It was all perfection required for being a soldier. The energy and vibe of Fort Campbell was something else. Every morning, every unit would be doing the PT and running for miles before 6 a.m. No one was allowed to sleep in, not even on the weekends. The level of commitment and dedication that everyone had was something that I had never seen before in my life. For me, it was doing the routine, going to the mess and then down to the motor pool.

Now ambulance driving was a whole new ball game and I had to come to terms with the ins and outs of it quickly. There are a lot of moving parts to an ambulance, quite literally. It's not just the vehicle itself but also the equipment that goes along with it. Every morning, we would perform the P.M.C.S., which is the Preventive Maintenance Checks and Services. This was to make sure that the ambulance was in good condition before we went out on a call. We would check the oil, the water, the tires and everything else. You are required to know the ambulance just like the back of your hand. The ambulance has to be functional at all times because you never know when you will get a call.

Now, as a medic, you could be assigned to a unit of soldiers in the field. That could be infantry, engineers, assault or any other number of units. You are responsible for the health and well-being of those soldiers. The unit I was with had three to six men and a helicopter unit. We were the ones that went to Desert Storm in 1991. Even today, in 2022, we have reunions at Fort Campbell to reminisce about the good old days. The camaraderie and brotherhood that we share is unbreakable.

We would be digging foxholes, using our bare hands if we had to, to get to the enemy. They were armpit deep, M16 by two. M16 is the length and width of your foxhole. You learn how to set up complete hospitals and have them up and running within 24 hours. You do this over and over again, in various locations and in various weather conditions. You learn how to set up wires and how to camouflage them. You learn how to camouflage yourself, your weapons and everything else. You learn how to move without making a sound, and you keep on practicing until you get it right. Fort Campbell makes you the best of the best. There is no other place like it in the world.

Before I go deeper, I need to explain how the organization of battalions work. Each battalion has four companies: Alpha, Bravo, Charlie and Delta. Each of these companies can have more than 100 men, and each man has his own specific job. There is a chain of command that everyone follows without question. The commanding officer is in charge of the entire battalion, and he has a second-in-command who is responsible for the day-to-day operations. These companies combined make a battalion, and then many battalions make up a brigade. So, when you are talking about an entire army, it is made up of many brigades.

So, back to 326 Medical Battalion. We had all these companies. The Delta company was the flight medics who would go out on the helicopters and provide medical care while in flight. The Charlie company was the ambulance unit with four to five squads of soldiers. Cooks and logistics made up the Bravo and Alpha companies. All the battalion would have to work like a well-oiled machine for everything to run smoothly. In that process, the entire cohesion becomes so strong that you would do anything for the guy next to you. You get to know the cooks, the supply people, the mechanics and everyone else in your battalion. They all reflect perfection in their own way and have a critical role to play.

Back then, being together day in and day out, we would do the daily grind together. During the training in the late 80s, we were making things perfect, but I had no idea that we were going to be called into action. I had never thought about it. I came in to be an army nurse and I would be out, right? Little did I know that the journey would take a turn. More on that in a while.

Through all of this perfection, discipline and training, your personal life doesn't stop here. You still have to maintain your own life, your children and everything else that comes with being in the army. You learn to be organized. So, in Fort Campbell with my two kids, God couldn't have been more kind at that time. Only a few months after we were assigned to Fort Campbell, Letty and her husband were assigned there from Germany too. So yeah, my babysitter was here, and my kids were happy. Ahmaad was 6 months while Rashad was two years old at that time.

True North

One of the greatest things that happened to me at Fort Campbell was New Birth, Jerusalem Church of God in Christ (COGIC). This was where I met Mother Cook, Pastor Cook and my big sister Dee. This God-given family was like a family to me. Sergeant Major Wilson, the epitome of a soldier, made me feel like I could do anything. Pastor

Cook taught me so much about life and how to love unconditionally. People around me at Fort Campbell made me feel accepted, and I soon realized that no matter where you go in the world, there is always a family waiting for you.

My journey through the military had made me a person of character. Therefore, I always carefully watched the people that were leading. To be a great leader, you must learn to follow great leaders. This is what Pastor Cook taught me and it has stuck with me throughout my life. I would also watch Mother Cook, who was the epitome of a prayer warrior. She taught me everything I needed to be taught: how to be a lady, how to be a woman of God, how to pray, how to depend on God, how to be a wife—you name it—and Mother Cook walked it, talked it, showed you and taught you.

This is also where I learned "true north" with Pastor Cook.

In the army, you learn how to read a compass and how to read a map. Back then, GPS was not around like it is today. So, you had to know how to triangulate your position by using a map and a compass. You had to calculate everything to understand where you had to be. So, when you read a map, there's a thing called grid north, magnetic north and true north. And they are all different.

Grid north is the north that is on the map that you have in your hand. It's the printed north. Every map has a little printed arrow somewhere on the map that tells you what direction is north. That's grid north. You can also call this the human north as it is the way we have learned to orient ourselves. Magnetic north is the north that a compass needle points to. The problem with magnetic north is that it changes. It's not constant. Being in different places on the earth, the magnetic north will point in different directions. So, different places and scenarios can be the magnetic north in your life.

And then we have true north. True north is God. Pastor Cook taught me that no matter where you go in this world, if you keep God as your true north, you will always find your way back home. So, this is something that I'm going to say was a download to me and it stuck out very much.

Dedication

As I moved through my journey with Fort Campbell, this was the place and the people I went to Desert Storm with. The five years spent there not only taught me how to be a soldier; it was also a time of personal growth. I learned how to be a woman of God, a woman of character and how to lead. I was able to take these lessons and use them throughout my life, no matter where the army sent me. The spiritual journey I took while at Fort Campbell has stayed with me and is still a part of me today.

How not to focus on the magnetic north but rather how to align with the true north, is something that I teach in my coaching. I thought the experience of Germany was soldier-like, but Fort Campbell was really where I became a woman and realized my potential. I learned how to make things happen as an NCO.

Chapter 5

Air Assault

"Women, like men, should try to do the impossible. And when they fall, their failure should be a challenge to others."
— Amelia Earhart

I had been to NCO school, been an ambulance driver and been a nurse in Germany. Now it was time to level up; it was time to become one of the Screaming Eagles. The 101st Airborne Division (Air Assault) is the best of the best, and being in Fort Campbell, Kentucky meant the next step in my career was nearby.

Once you're in Fort Campbell, it becomes impossible not to go to an air assault school or become a paratrooper. There's a slight difference between the two. In air assault, jumping out of the helicopter comes with the aid of a rope. In paratrooper school, you're just jumping out of the plane with a chute on your back and hoping for the best. I chose air assault.

The Challenge of a Female Officer

An air assault school is a two-week process. And once you get that patch—the coveted black and yellow 101st Airborne Division patch— you're a part of an elite group. The school was a totally different experience. It doesn't matter if you're a male or a female; you will be treated the same. You're all green and there to learn how to properly wear the rucksack, set up an LZ (landing zone) and repel down a ropes course. The intensity of the course doesn't differentiate between genders.

Here's a YouTube video I found that will give you an idea of what air assault school is like:

Anyway, at school, I had a really good time. This can mainly be attributed to a young private from my squad, whom I took under my wing. The young lad was full of character. He was the main provider of his family, and there was nothing he wouldn't do to become the best soldier he could be. So, with him along for the journey, how could I not have a good time?

Something to Prove

Because I had passed the NCO school previously, I was a Sergeant NCO. And as they say, NCOs make it happen. So, for an NCO like me, not passing the air assault school wasn't an option. We had to do an obstacle course, followed right after by a 2-mile run. Finishing it within the time meant that we could then enter the air assault group. We learned how to sling and load equipment, how to air assault into areas, and so on and so on. It was very intense training and we had to run everywhere. We had to do a lot of push-ups and a lot of physical training. Every time your left foot would hit the ground, you would run the entire time you were there. On the last day of the course, there was a 12-mile ruck march that we had to complete within 3 hours. Only then would you be considered an air assault graduate.

So yes, I made it. I am now an air assault graduate. It felt like such a complete sense of accomplishment—being one with nature and being able to conquer anything that was put in front of me. I was now a part of an elite group and I had earned it. The things I learned and the experiences I had during those two weeks, I will never forget.

So now, at Fort Campbell, I still remember the captain of our unit: an intense man, full of vigor and excellence. He demanded the same of us. It was tough but we had to do what we had to do. There were early mornings and late nights, but it was all worth it in the end.

Luckily, I had my favorite Sergeant Major Wilson. Under him, I became a re-enlistment NCO. NCOES (Non-Commissioned Officer Education System) is a great way to learn more about what it means to be an NCO. Working here, under Sergeant Major Wilson, I was able to learn more about the army. It came with some privileges too.

The work was basically talking to soldiers, motivating and convincing them and getting them to understand why re-enlisting in the army was a good idea. I was pretty good at it too, if I do say so myself. I was also involved with legal affairs such as court-martials and non-judicial punishments. It was all a learning experience along with lots of clerical work. But it gave me a better understanding of how the army works from the inside.

Dope on a Rope

Under such a competent leader, there was no way I wasn't going to be air assault qualified and excel in my work. Once you become air assault qualified, they give you a special name: "dope on a rope."

So, by now, as my uniform goes and with my awards, I was now an ambulance driver, a Screaming Eagle with the 101st Airborne Division and an air assault qualified "dope on a rope." What was next for me?

Chapter 6

The Invasion

"The ultimate measure of a man is not where he stands in moments of convenience and support, but where he stands at times of challenge and controversy."
– Martin Luther King, Jr.

August 2, 1990—I will not forget this moment in my life.

Life in Fort Campbell was quite simple and sweet by now. I had learned to be the soldier I was content with. I had nailed the precision and dedication. Life was a routine: wake up in the morning, get the kids ready and to the babysitter, get to the base, do my PT and go off for breakfast at the hall.

I had always been a big breakfast person—fried potatoes, biscuits, orange juice and grits with cheese—something that would befit the amount of duty and responsibility I had to put in for the day. A big breakfast would keep me energized as it was going to be either the motor pool with the ambulance and doing missions, or out in the field with the unit. The soldiering life was one I loved. Alongside this, I was also working as the re-enlistment NCO. With that came a lot of duties. The clerical work did make my love for computers blossom.

Okay, so, it's August the 2nd, 1990; I'm at home watching TV with my husband. It was a Thursday night, and we were just relaxing. And then the news flashed. Saddam Hussein had invaded Kuwait. I remember being in shock as I watched the images of the tanks rolling into Kuwait City. It looked like a scene from a movie, but it was real.

We knew that this was not going to be good. Well, guess what? We were in the army and, more specifically, the 101st Airborne. So, we knew that things were about to get real.

Activation

At 101st, there is always a battalion and brigade that is ready to be deployed at any given time. The cycle rotates so that every unit gets a chance to be the ready brigade. So, you have to be prepared to be deployed within 48 hours' notice. And that is exactly what happened. Once a bridge gets activated, it's action. You can't take a leave; you can't go on a pass or anything. You report to your unit and await further instructions. When our brigade got the call, the training and preparation began immediately. We had to be ready for anything and everything.

Desert Storm was the first time where both husbands and wives were deployed together. There was no time to reassign units or for people to request not to deploy. The army doesn't work like that. You go where you're needed and that's that. Women would serve in all areas during Desert Storm. There were women on the front lines, flying helicopters, driving tanks and working in support roles. Previously, a role largely restricted to the medical field was no longer the case.

Getting Ready

So, as you can imagine, it was a very chaotic and stressful time for families. Some women were getting pregnant to avoid deployment. There were soldiers who were deliberately injuring themselves to get out of going. It's not easy to go to someplace where you don't know if you'll come back alive.

But as soldiers, we know the risks. And it was a very hard decision. Everett and I talked too long about it. But for me, it was clear. I learned character, responsibility and dedication. I learned how to soldier. How could I not go and serve my country when it needed me the most? I had joined the army to be a nurse, though, something I wasn't still close to yet; but even then, my duty was to serve. So, I signed up. I did what soldiers do. We do missions and we complete them.

So now, because we were going, we had to activate a plan for our children too. Everett and I were both in Fort Campbell, so there was a possibility that both of us could be deployed, and we had to make sure that our children were well taken care of in our absence. We made the decision to put them in the care of my mother. Both Rashad and Ahmaad would be going to live with her. I'd send the money for their care and everything, but it was going to be a big adjustment for all of us.

Get Set

So, within a week, my mom came and took the boys back to Columbus, Ohio. Everett's mother and my mother would take turns watching the boys. Lucky for us, we had my mom's church, Mt. Olivet Baptist Church, and Everett's mother's church, Triedstone Baptist Church, to help with childcare and support. It was a community effort and we all pulled together to make it work. Not to forget, Rosemont School for Girls chipped in too. So, there were lots of people who would help to make sure that our children were okay. But as a mother, it was the hardest thing I've ever had to do in my life—leaving my children behind and not knowing when I would see them again.

Go

The training at Fort Campbell was intense. We had to be ready for anything. The entire base was on lockdown. You couldn't leave; you couldn't do anything. All you could do was train, and that's what we did. Packing and loading up the equipment took a lot of time too. But eventually, we were ready, and it was time to go.

Now for me, Germany had been quite an experience, but Kuwait was going to be a whole different story. The temperature was going to be a lot and there was going to be sand everywhere. We thought Fort Jackson and Fort Sam Houston were hot, but Kuwait was going to be a different level of hot.

So, with goodbyes said and a promise to return, we boarded the plane and headed out, not knowing what the future held but knowing that we had to be strong for our country, our families and ourselves.

Chapter 7

Tent City

*"I hate war as only a soldier who has lived it can,
only as one who has seen its brutality,
its futility, its stupidity."*
– Dwight D. Eisenhower

After completing our training, it was time to go. I wasn't sure what to expect, but I knew it wasn't going to be easy. We had trained at Fort Campbell, and if you recall earlier in the book, I mentioned how huge it actually is. The 101st Airborne Division is unique in that it covers two states—Kentucky and Tennessee—and four cities, those being Hopkinsville, Fort Campbell, Clarksville and Nashville. This means that the soldiers who serve in this division can be from either state.

It was in the back of Fort Campbell where we could do training and a bulk load of practice; and not only there, but we also went out in the field and practiced setting up our combat medical support hospital. This is to tell you that the battalion there is always full of a completely operational unit that is functional all the time.

The battalion at Fort Campbell is a very special unit. It has soldiers who can do medical, dental and surgical work, so you get these facilities while you train there. There are also cooks and people who work in logistics and supply. We also had our Delta unit, which was full of snipers, and they were a huge asset to our battalion. We had a helicopter medical team and a helicopter mechanics team. There were mechanics for all the vehicles and the motor pool. This was a huge plus for us; in transportation, our helicopters were always in top condition.

So, basically, we had everything up and running and fully operational. With the training and equipment that we had, it was time to test them and ourselves now. It was time to deploy. It was time to leave Campbell for King Fahd and Kuwait.

Arrival at King Fahd Airport

Now, as we prepared to leave for Kuwait, we had made up our minds about the weather. We knew we were going to be in a desert climate, and it was important to be prepared for the harsh conditions. We also had understood and trained for everything that we could face there, but were we ready? Anyway, we flew.

We were flown into Kuwait and landed at King Fahd airport. From there, we were transported to our new training area. This was necessary despite our previous training as we were in a new land, Saudi Arabia, of course. We had to go through some training and understanding of the area that we were in. We needed to understand the laws and regulations there. The weather was different than what we were used to, and it was important to know what to expect.

We set up our tents in places to stay. It was difficult as we even had to secure showers and build bathrooms ourselves. But we did, and we eventually became a well-oiled machine. It was important to be prepared for anything that we might encounter. There are some unique things that I don't think most people know about deploying to deserts. The "desert storm" is the first war you deal with, and it was a whole different monster than what we were used to, which took some getting used to.

Acclimatization

The first thing worth mentioning is that all female soldiers had to cut their hair prior to deployment. You could not board the airplane without cutting your hair, and this was for several reasons. The first reason was not knowing what our water sources were going to be. It is a fact that it takes much more time and a lot of water for women to shower and shampoo their hair, especially if they have long hair. Another reason was that we didn't want anything obstructing our vision or getting caught in any machinery. It's also much harder to keep your hair clean and free of sand and dirt in a desert environment. You cannot blow dry it and take care of it as you don't have all those amenities, so it was evident and necessary that everyone had to cut their hair.

It was difficult for many of us. I recall our lieutenant in the personnel division, who had long red hair, and I want to say that it came all the way down her back, and to cut her hair was an ordeal. I did not have long hair like her, but I was not prepared to cut my hair either. Unfortunately, it was something we had to do to make it easy to maintain. This was because, as said earlier, we didn't know what situation we would find ourselves in and what our water supply was going to be.

As a matter of fact, water was so scarce, it was brought to us in little amounts and put in some tubs. These tubs were then suspended over a wooden structure that would allow us to go and shower. More on this will be explained later.

After some time, we understood a couple of things about Kuwait and Saudi Arabia, one of which was that no Bibles were allowed. Although we carried Bibles with us, we could not display those openly. We did have Bible study and church services, but it was inside our hangers and within our area, and that was from our chaplain in the military. Secondly, there was no alcohol for us as well.

Women in War

Among us female soldiers, those who wanted to could get some laundry done by buying a service. You could also wash your own clothes out with a bucket and soap and hang them up to dry outside your tent. But all this was to be done while keeping in mind that women were not to be in roles of leadership and show that. We had to keep our arms covered all the time. It was very difficult to get our lingerie washed. We could not wash and display our underclothes, so there was a time period when we had to resort to wearing brown boxers, which is what everybody would wear then—just brown boxers and a t-shirt, or occasionally a sports bra. Hence, there were challenges that we had to go through that you don't really think about normally. Surviving in the desert is never easy.

An interesting thing about when we landed was finding our way. We had to go by bus to where we were to be located. And again, as you know, this was in 1990. So, there were neither cellphones nor GPS. It was just you looking at a map and using a landmark. Landmarks in a desert, you say? There's nothing in the desert but white and fine sand. I recall riding that bus when we first got there, which was nothing near to a normal ride. Not too far after we got on that bus, we had to have the bus driver pull off the side of the road, and males and females would get out to use the bathroom on the side of the road. This was because we had been drinking a lot of water to try to stay hydrated due to the high temperatures. There was nothing else that we could do because we were instructed to drink ample amounts of water in order to help prevent dehydration.

Men serving side by side with women was very difficult. At this point, I want to remind you that this was the first time that we had women in all types of assignments, serving with husbands. I know that some of the men that I attended church with, at Fort Campbell, used to check on me regularly as they were worried about me and cared for me. I was like a sister to them and, for some, a mother.

It becomes difficult to lose people in war when you have developed a bond like that. You care for one another, not just as comrades in arms but as sisters and brothers in the Lord. This is the type of people that you want beside you when things get tough. So, it's very hard to know that that person could get injured or could lose their life. And we did have women, who we knew, lose their lives.

One thing I did was to take a sock from Ahmaad, my youngest son, when I left. He was two and Rashad was four. I had left them with my parents and my ex-husband's parents. It was hard to leave my children behind when I had to go. But as a mother, I knew it was important that I do my job. So, I took something with me from each of them to hold on to. God knows I kept praying that I would come back to the United States and see my children again.

Here I was, having landed in a whole new world. Although it was a completely strange place, I had a battle buddy with me. She was stationed in Alaska. One very interesting thing about her is that when she came into the military, she was able to join at a late stage in her life. Therefore, she's now an older woman with several heart conditions. It was especially hard for her, given that we used to eat MREs. We had to carry everything in our rucksack, which was heavy. So, there were a lot of instances when I would have to help her carry her load, especially if we had to run off of a plane or run onto a plane because we were going from point A to point B.

Even in war, we ran PT. The military is always looking for ways to improve the physical fitness of their soldiers. That way, when we are in a combat situation, we are able to perform better. We got up early and ran for two to four miles on a daily basis to be in perfect shape at all times, and because we had to get acclimated to the weather as well. We had a similar routine back in Fort Campbell and in the United States. We would do the same in war: get up, read, do PT and go to the mess hall to eat.

As for eating, in the beginning, we only ate MREs, which are meals that are ready to eat. My favorite was the wieners, which were somewhat like Vienna sausages back in the day, or the peanut butter or the cheese spread. You do get creative, and you also get bored after eating MREs for months, but that would not call for a change in what you got to eat.

Back then, we had been medics, as you are aware. This meant shifting and moving to and from hospitals, sometimes in the middle of the night, trying to get patients the care they needed. So sometimes, when taking a soldier to a local hospital for an emergency, you may get to stop at places, look around, inquire and get other things.

For example, on the side of the road, there was always a gentleman grilling chicken, which now I understand was not the smartest idea. How can one keep chicken fresh in the scorching heat of a 100-degree temperature on the side of the road, in a small grill like that? But I can't tell you how many times I stopped and partook of that "chicken with a piece of pita." Reasons like that could be why a lot of soldiers came back from the war with parasites and other things.

We indulged in things like that and many others, as a lot of us didn't think that we would make it back. Once you think like that, you do things that you probably wouldn't do when under conditions of war. Of course, we had showers that were built, and these showers were located in the middle of tent city so that everyone could use them. They would get filled with water on a regular basis.

I was an NBC officer (i.e., nuclear, biological and chemical warfare). As an NBC officer, you are responsible for a lot of things. I also was assigned to be the NBC, NCO, which entailed training and making sure we had equipment and protocols in place, in case of a nuclear weapons attack. In addition, I frequently conducted safety inspections to ensure compliance with all safety protocols, and surveillance to make sure we were prepared for chemical attacks. So, there were times when we had to wear our masks. We also had to pull guard duty. Everyone was required to pull their fair share to stand guard to protect the gates.

Will You Survive?

The military burned the toilet areas with gas. We used diesel and mogas, the fuel that was used for our vehicles. This was to get rid of the smell and to stop any diseases from spreading. As soldiers, we would get assigned the task to burn the urine and feces. It's called the burn pit. You would be responsible for pouring gas, which was mogas and diesel. The job included tearing down the toilet area and the latrine, pouring gas over it and burning it, until it was all burned. That would take hours, and we didn't even have any masks on. It was an assignment that was rotated. And when it was your turn, you had to perform that duty. There was no running from the things that needed to take place for survival.

All women would stay in their tents. It was our home, and we took care of it. There will be photos where you can see how we decorated our tent. We used to get care packages from students and teachers and groups of churches, who would send things over for soldiers. Those packages also included toiletries and snack items. The lovely people made sure that we were well taken care of and tried to help us feel like it was home as much as possible.

An amazing thing to add was that CSM Wilson built Ocea and me an office. It was really nice. This was a credit to CSM Wilson, who took care of us, mainly because you always have sandstorms and windstorms there. And I tell you, when that sand came through, especially if you had just gotten out of the shower, it was definitely not fun to be covered in it.

So, as you can imagine, the sand would get in all of your clothes, and you can't shower every day in a war. It's not like you could just go to the store and buy some shampoo or soap. You had to make do with what you had. Although you could sometimes take a shower on a daily basis, you often had to make it through those daily challenges. Many women chose to get rid of their hair during or before deployments because it was one less thing to worry about. Hair can be a nuisance in the desert, especially when it's windy or dusty and you are unable to clean it, so lots of women would lose gobs of hair.

We lost a lot of soldiers to friendly fire. That's one of the dangers of being in the military. You never know when or how you're going to die. It could be from a disease, it could be from an illness, it could be from the enemy or it could be from our own troops. People boarded before the actual war started; they were there in preparation mode, playing with their weapons and playing with the law. Some even committed suicide. The suicide rate was very high, so more lives were being lost than just in the war.

I believe Desert Storm was the shortest war. From the time that it actually started, to the end, it may have been one of the shortest wars, but I can say that we lost a lot of soldiers to these accidents.

As a soldier, you have to be willing to do whatever it takes to protect your country. Guard duty is no joke and it's something that all soldiers are required to do. As I have mentioned, we did guard duty as well. I recall an incident especially related to a lieutenant; I believe his name was Lieutenant Blankenship. When we were on guard duty, he would like to play games to see if we were alert and prepared. I didn't think it was funny as he would even play those games in situations when we had a loaded M16. I made sure to let him know that this could go wrong really quick. But it was all in vain. Anyway, as time went on, he matured and stopped playing those games.

What else was there to do in a 100-degree temperature environment in the middle of the desert? One task we had to do was watch each other sleep. This was because you had to make sure that your buddy drank fluid and stayed hydrated. They would do the same for you if you slept, and they would watch you, staying awake themselves. Your neighbor would wake you up to make sure you drank water, and you would then allow them to sleep.

In the mornings, we used to get up really early, like five or six, before the sun came up and before it became really hot. Only then, after completing our work, would we be required to go back and stay in our tents to try our best to stay cool. We would report back to work when the sun went down. It would continue like that, and if you think about how Alaska is and the reflection from the sun and moon on the white sand, or this "white snow," it's almost like you're in a different world. It was definitely a sight to see. There were some other things that were very unique to me. In the war, there was the creation of the showers, the bathrooms, having no privacy, etc., but that will be explained later, when I give you some extras.

It was definitely not easy being away from him and my family. Fortunately, I was able to see my husband a couple of times, only because he was a combat engineer. Therefore, he operated heavy equipment and built roads, bridges and other things of that nature. For that reason, he was on the road a lot. So, he was able to find where I was located and sometimes visit, and we could see each other for brief moments. Otherwise, we had to mainly write letters to each other, even though we were both in Saudi Arabia.

One of the interesting things about living in a military town is that you have a full functioning city. You have all the amenities that you would find in any other city. Another was the fact that we didn't have cell phones or email. We were unable to communicate with the outside world in the way that we were used to. We had to rely on letter-writing packages and mail clerks.

Apart from those, I used to send cassette tapes. I would record a tape of me talking, so that my kids could hear and remember my voice. I used to randomly talk for an hour and send it back home. Gladly, my mom would do the same thing and engage the kids in talking so that I could hear their voices. She would send me that tape to play in order to help minimize my homesickness and the sadness from not having my children around.

I recall a couple of other unique things that I experienced. For example, before we were moved to Kuwait, we lived in what we used to call "Tent City." This was most of Fort Campbell because we were all living in tents, and it was nothing but a big city of tents where everyone performed their jobs in excellence. We all lived there in unity and did what we were supposed to do until we were required to move forward.

I remember the evening clearly when the sirens went off and the war started. I remember the intense moment and the anxiety it caused in all of us who were in their tents. We didn't know what to expect, but we knew it was going to be something big. We could hear the bombs going off and we knew that we had to be prepared. One could see the sky lighting up. Amidst all that, being medics, you never knew when you would be called to rescue someone or when you would have to leave and head out onto the battlefield. We could also be called to get someone who fainted due to heat exhaustion or just got injured.

Anyhow, we survived, and we were able to get together. We would have Bible studies to keep each other going. There are some other unique things that took place and, again, those will be disclosed later.

Home Sweet Home

Our tenure in Kuwait lasted from September 1990 to April 1991. We were there in Kuwait, serving in Desert Storm.

It was an amazing and wonderful thing when we were allowed to prepare to come home, by starting to clean our equipment. We were all excited and could not wait to go back to our families and loved ones. We knew that there were going to be a lot of changes awaiting us. Not only did we have to clean and pack all of our gear, but we had to really get rid of the sand that we were never going to take home. So, we had to clean the equipment and our personal gear, maybe 10 or 15 times, in order to be permitted to fly back. We managed to do it and finally got home.

I will never forget the flight and seeing the United States for the first time. It was so beautiful, and I could not believe that I was finally home. Being back in our own country, with our own people, felt so good. The intensity on the plane—the screams, the yells—was something unexplainable. I think when we got off that plane, most of us hit the ground and could not believe we had made it home.

We survived.

Chapter 8

Overseas Again—Really?

*"Motherhood is the greatest thing
and the hardest thing."*
– Ricki Lake

We made it back to the United States. We were finally able to be with our families and loved ones after being away for so long. We came back from Fort Campbell, the large base containing several battalions and brigades. Despite the fact that we were happy to be home, there were still a lot of changes awaiting us. Soldiers had been gone from September 1990 to April 1991.

We obviously had to go through some briefings. This was a good thing for us, on how to go back to our families and acclimate with our children and spouses who were not serving in the war. The spouses of the soldiers were given a briefing on how to interact with their family members. They were briefed on the different ways that they may have changed since they had been away. The spouses were also given information on how to handle the returning soldiers.

If the stats from those years were checked, there were so many cases of homicides, suicides and divorces. There was so much going on, which was probably par for the course of war because husbands would think wives had been unfaithful and vice versa. People just realized that they didn't have steel mesh, and we were no different. Imagine a situation where you get back and you're given a mandatory 21 days off to go to your hometown and see your family and relax.

A great thing about going home was also the fact that my husband and I flew in on the exact same day, which is very rare to happen. Our units had flown out of Saudi on the exact same day, although at different times. I can't seem to remember who arrived first at Fort Campbell, but I do remember that both families had driven down from Columbus to greet us coming back from the war. Anyway, we had gotten back, and even though we had seen each other a few times during the war, they were very brief meetings. The majority of the time, we were not assigned close enough to each other. As a result, we wrote letters to each other in addition.

We got back and we, of course, stayed in a hotel room because Everett had put our house up for rent while we were away, and there was another family living in our house. Therefore, after our stay at the hotel, we moved to Columbus, Ohio for those 21 days, for evident reasons. While we were there, I thought it was just right that we appreciated and say thank you to those people that wrote letters and sent care packages to us; in addition, those who helped with our children, my mom's church and his mom's church and numerous family members and friends that supported us during the war.

The Breakup

After having all that done, we were just about ready to go back to Fort Campbell when Everett came home and gave me a piece of news. He told me that he had heard a pastor preach and he was then thinking that he had married the wrong woman. He wanted to get a divorce, and he wanted to go back to his ex from high school, where he had two children. The news was shocking, but I told him I was okay with that. If you recall from the beginning, you know that I'm a little bit of a chicken. I'm not a big fighter, and I don't like confrontation.

Now that I'm in my 50s, if I look back at it, I would say that we got married too soon. We were aware that absence makes the heart grow fonder. Well, it should have worked for us as we both had been apart, wanting to work for the military, but it was still a lot less than love for us. So, there we were, with two children, having been home for 21 days to live together, and we ended up breaking up.

There are so many soldiers who would tell stories of families and fights, which I was not going to do at all. Hence, I accepted that with an "Okay" and came back to Fort Campbell. At Fort Campbell, I got my own place and brought my two boys, whereas he moved to the barracks.

I went to my sergeant major and told him, "Sergeant Major! I think I might be pregnant." I shall never forget CSM Wilson, who said, "Sergeant Fields, you don't get paid to think." I told the major that we had been at war for so long and I wasn't taking any birth control, but he would not believe my words.

But lo and behold, exactly nine months after getting back from the desert, came what Fort Campbell put in the paper as "Desert Storm Nestlings." Fort Campbell was having a record-bursting nine months post-war. There were so many births that they had to call in air force doctors to come and help deliver babies. So, then came son number 3, Isaiah. The interesting thing about Isaiah's birth was that he was

73

born on his dad's birthday. It was astounding, and "wow" was all I could say to that.

I was now a single parent. This meant that I had to take care of my three boys by myself. There was Sergeant Major Wilson and his wife. She ran the hospital at Fort Campbell. That did not mean that she was a combat field medic; she just ran the hospital. CSM Wilson decided that it was time for me to get out of the field unit. This meant that I would stop jumping out of helicopters and go work at Blanchfield Army Hospital, Fort Campbell, Kentucky. Eventually, I went to meet CSM Wilson and his wife to get reassigned.

Reassignment

As my new designation, I got assigned to the emergency room. This was, of course, very good for me because my purpose to come into the army was to be an "army nurse," and what better training could there be than at the emergency room at Fort Campbell, Kentucky?

This was a trauma emergency room, and I was always working because anything that happens in Tennessee, Kentucky, and many areas close by, was being brought here. This meant that I was getting trained on how to handle different types of traumas. Another great thing was that we had helicopter medics, which would mean that they could fly over to areas of any accidents and work on the traumas on the spot. This increased the efficiency of the care provided by us, which was all a good aspect of the job.

The only negative aspect was that I was assigned the night shift. A night shift with three boys was a major problem for me. I guess this is where the army again says, "We didn't issue you those kids," or "Your children are not the army's problem." I loved the emergency room, so it was solely my responsibility to figure out how to make that work when working third shift, and still be able to take care of my children. That was one of the hardest things I have ever had to do.

The Scare

In March 1992, after being back in my homeland and having Isaiah born in January of 1992, and keeping up with work, I got a scare. For some time, I had something bothering me in my throat. I decided to go to the hospital and get some tests performed. After multiple tests and a biopsy, the news was broken to me that I had thyroid cancer. I was informed that I needed to get surgery and have my thyroid removed. This was both devastating and a shock to me. I felt like I had been hit by a truck. I did not want to have surgery. To me, I was a member of the New Birth. I just could not believe that I had thyroid cancer. I said, "This is not possible."

This was when the major, who had broken the news to me, called the colonel of our battalion and informed him that I was refusing to go and have surgery. Believe it or not, I got called in, and the colonel said to me, "Sergeant Fields! I know you to be a woman of faith and a religious one, but you do not belong to yourself. You belong to Uncle Sam." He gave me two choices: Either I got the surgery or I would have to get out of the military. He was so stern that I could not avoid the surgery while my tests showed thyroid cancer. How could I have not given in to that? I had to have the surgery, so I decided to get it.

I had wonderful people around me, including Mother Cook and Pastor Cook, who supported me and helped take care of the boys while I prepared for the surgery. The interesting thing was, after I had the surgery and I woke up post-surgery, I found the major sitting in my room, along with Mother Cook, who never left my side. I shall never forget that she stayed right there for the whole time.

Back then, thyroid surgery was very delicate. If they touched an area like the parathyroid, or there was just a small error, that could cause your throat to close. There could be many post-operational complications, so even after you had woken up, you had a nurse assigned to your bed to monitor you for the first 24 hours.

The major said to me, "We got your thyroid out and we sent it to the lab for testing, and we found no cancer." There was no cancer. It was like a part of what we do in the military: We accomplish the mission, we suck it up and we drive on, because it's done now. At least they didn't take all of the thyroid but just part of the thyroid.

Following that, I had to go through recovery, which went pretty well for a significant time, except that in September of 92, I heard a pop in my neck. I was just sitting in the living room and my neck popped open. It was so bad that I had to go through another surgery. It was followed by a series of infections. My body was rejecting the sutures, and it led to the formation of an abscess, which I had to have removed. I ended up having a hole in my neck, and the hole was so big that it looked like I'd had a tracheostomy. Long story short, I resumed my work in the ER and allowed my body to heal.

Make a Choice

Before 1992 ended, I got an assignment to go back to Germany. I turned the orders down for obvious reasons. I was having so much to deal with. My body was not healing properly from the thyroid surgery. I wondered how they could send me to Germany. I was a single mom with three sons. There was no way I could go there. So, I did not accept the orders and, two months later, I had orders again. I was needed in Germany. I was dazed; I could not understand it and definitely could not believe it.

Then I was struck by the forced realization again that, "Those children are not the army's issue. You chose to have those children." Then, I had to make a choice. I had to decide. Was I going back to Germany, overseas again—really? This time, there was no turning down the orders; they came up and I was scheduled to go to Mannheim, Germany to work in a prison. I thought to myself, "Is this the assignment that will get me closer to becoming an army nurse?"

Chapter 9

That's All Folks; I'm Done

*"Now this is not the end. It is not even
the beginning of the end. But it is, perhaps,
the end of the beginning."*
– Winston Churchill

Second Deployment

I had to start to prepare for Germany, so that's what I did. The hole in my neck was still there; only by then it had turned into a fistula and, every now and then, a suture would come out of it. I had a hard time as it was a visible hole again and, most of the time, there was pus coming out. It again looked like I had had a tracheostomy.

"How can I go to Germany with three sons?" I pondered. "Will I ever decide to get out of the military?" No. At that time, I decided I did not want to. Although I was still a married woman at that time, as we had not officially gotten divorced—we were just separated—that did not mean that I could deploy to Germany and have Everett as my dependent, especially while knowing that he was living with his former girlfriend, who also happened to be the mother of his two children.

It was 1993, and Isaiah was a year old and (AJ) Ahmaad was five, whereas Rashad had reached seven years of age. I could not figure out how I was going to go to Germany with my three sons. It was time, and I had to pull myself together and make that flight. I had to go over and find housing in Germany. Most importantly, I needed to find a babysitter and get ready to start our life over there.

Friedberg, Germany

I was going to be assigned to Friedberg this time. Friedberg, Germany is especially known for where Elvis Presley served in the military, right outside of Frankfurt. For those who do not know, Elvis Presley was an American singer and actor. He was one of the most popular musicians of the 20th century. He served in the military for several years. He was stationed in Germany for two of those years.

Tank Duty

I had thought to myself that I was going to be the medic at the prison, which would get me closer to my nursing, but this was not the case at all. I was brought to Frankfurt as a double-patched Screaming Eagle—an air assault, sharpshooting sergeant from "101st Airborne Screaming Eagles." Unlike my anticipation of my designation, when I got to Frankfurt, I was told that I was needed at the tank unit. "Tank unit?" I was startled. "Do we have women driving tanks?" I inquired. My inquiry was answered: "Yes, we do! And you're going to the 501st FSB, to be attached to the 1st Armored Division."

This could not be happening—1st Armored Division! Were they serious? It turned out that they were very much so. It was settled, and I was diverted to a new unit in Friedberg, Germany. I was in the 501st FSB (Forward Support Battalion) tank unit, driving at 113. To my surprise, I was up for it, and I absolutely loved it.

I left my children in Philadelphia with my dad's sister, signed the power of attorney and asked her to watch my three children. Meanwhile, I would go to Germany and sort things out, like finding housing and getting set up. I chose to do that because it was easier to fly in and out of Philadelphia, as an international flight to Germany, than it was to come all the way back to Columbus. To my gratitude, my aunt Renee and Uncle Sam agreed to take care of my three boys until I could get situated myself.

Having that taken care of, I had to come back for the divorce court. I had applied for a divorce, but in Columbus, Ohio, you also have to attend divorce sessions before your divorce is granted. You have to go to these sessions and be there in person; however, Everett did not appear. They published the request in the paper for four weeks. Since he was not to be seen in one, I was granted my divorce. After divorce school, I took a flight to Philadelphia, picked up my sons and flew off to Butzbach, Germany. That was what we called home for the next two years.

The interesting thing about being in a tank unit is that when you support a tank unit, you're always in the field. Every 60 days or say 90 days, you're being deployed somewhere because there's always an artillery unit going out for training. There were two training areas in Germany: Hohenfels and Grafenwoehr. At the present time, there are eleven training areas in Germany in total. This means that you are always on the move. Anyway, both these areas were like the back of Fort Campbell areas where we would go and drive the tanks. We could also set up our hospital there. As tank units, we were attached to the

Bradley so that if they were down, we could get in and get the soldiers out and back to safety.

In contrast to that, our tank was a little bit smaller. We carried four gurneys in our tank, and it would serve just like an ambulance. As mentioned earlier, I just loved the whole experience of being in a tank and serving in the field. It gave me a thrill and I loved it. At the times when we were not out in the field, I ran a clinic on a small base that the Armored Division occupied. On that base, there were only a few females. I ran the clinic that processed all soldiers coming into that base and going out of it. This was what I had always wanted to do. A thing to be noted here is that we didn't have a doctor on the base, so I would just confer with the doctor about the patients. He would review my charting, but it was me who ran the lab. I did all testing and saw all the clients. As a result, I was enjoying it, as this job was really getting me closer to my nursing if not being a doctor.

I was still assigned to the tank; therefore, not much of my enjoyment had occurred when it came around that we had to start training for Bosnia. I was not too sure if I wanted to go to Bosnia, and not even sure if I wanted to leave my kids again. Meanwhile, at Frankfurt, and being assigned to the tank, we used to have times when we were guaranteed that we would not have to go to the field. Hence, I sent for my mom, my aunt Barbara Ruth and my niece Tiffany, to come and visit us in Germany for two weeks. And as one could expect in my journey, we got put on alert to deploy to Bosnia, while they all were there visiting us.

What could one do then to prepare to deploy and get out to the field? Eventually, I had to leave my mom and my aunt in the great care of my babysitter. The good thing was that they were now with the boys, whereas my team and I were deployed out to the field to start training.

We got some eye-opening lessons during our training as we were annihilated in less than 30 minutes in all our sessions. This was partly due to some new soldiers who were not seasoned. There were always a lot of new soldiers joining the army, so there had been an influx of new soldiers who may not have been trained the way we were trained at Fort Campbell.

One day while I was training for Bosnia, I got a call from my babysitter, who told me that my boys had come to a decision. They wanted to go back to America with my mom. She told me she could loan me enough money for my mom to take the boys back, and that I could pay her back whenever. She had casually told me, and it was so much to process. I was out in the field, preparing for Bosnia, while my kids were homesick and wanted to go back to the States with their grandmother. My babysitter knew I was good for the money. She bought their tickets, and they went away from me. I was as confused and speechless as one can imagine. I didn't know what I was going to do. I didn't know what to think.

The Attack

I had also started dating a "gentleman"; let us call him DH. What a gentleman... When I came back from training, he broke into my apartment. I had a Rottweiler at home named Karina, and a rabbit as well. Although I think it was the rabbit who ruled between them, the Rottweiler had special authority. Anyway, having both of them there, I still woke up with DH in my apartment—not just having broken in but attempting to choke me as well. He had desperation in his eyes and was choking me with all his might, and he was threatening me to marry him or else he would harm me as well as my children.

Things got as weird as they could get, leaving me with no clue what had happened. I could not think of what possibly had caused him to be so aggressive. I somehow managed to get free from his attack, and only after that, I realized something. Earlier during her visit, my mom had brought over some pictures and memorabilia of my ex-husband for the boys to see. DH got his hands on them, and his jealousy got the best of him. He thought that I was reminiscing about my ex-husband and got enraged at the thought of that. His reasoning, his act and his intent were so intense and dangerous that I felt I had no choice but to report it to the military police.

While talking to my family, who were back in America, I explained what had happened, and there was a unanimous and most predictable reaction from them. All three of them together asked me to just get out of there. To me, there were many things a person could do in such situations, but I had not thought of this. I had to acknowledge their feelings and understand their perspective—to see it from their eyes, how their mom had gone to war, and when she came back, they got separated from their dad and had to live in Germany.

Germany for them was not that bad; in fact, it was great. We had lived a brief but good life in Germany, and the kids loved it there too. It was safe and warm. I tried to provide them with the best too. I made sure to keep them in the German economy. We had great babysitters who took care of them. They had wonderful friends with whom they used to play, friends that they still know to this day.

Apart from that, there were some turndowns as well. Being assigned to the tank unit, their mom was not available most of the time. I recall I would put Isaiah to sleep one night, and then in the morning, I would be gone—not just gone; I had to be away for 30 days or sometimes even 40. It was so hard for the little guy. Whenever I called home to talk to the boys, my babysitter would tell me that I could talk to Rashad or Ahmaad but not Isaiah, as he might not take it well.

Isaiah was two years of age, given that it was 1994 and 1995 when we were in Germany. He could never tell if his mom was going to be at home with him or if she would be gone for days. Considering his age and sentiments, talking to him over the phone would make it more difficult to adjust.

Thus, being a tank driver was not an easy task. One moment you are laughing with your kids, and the next morning you are gone. Not to repeat the same motto that "the children are not the army's issue," but the army has nothing to do with your family. Our uniform, our boots and our equipment is army-issue, not our families. It was then up to me to stand up and have the responsibility of taking care of my children. Guess what? This time, I did that. I gave in. It was especially after the DH incident that I told my boys, "I am going to be released from the army." It was time to let it go.

It was challenging to be a single mom and to serve along with that. It was especially hard being an Air Assault 101st Screaming Eagle. Hooray! There it was; I had made the decision to get out and to return to the civilian world.

Chapter 10

The Return to Civilian World

"There is nothing either good or bad but thinking makes it so."
– William Shakespeare

What was I thinking? I had thought so much about becoming an army nurse. I wanted to be able to take care of my family and serve my country at the same time. My aim in being an army nurse was to get up early and do more before 9 a.m. than most people do all day. But life always has other plans for you. So, there I was, 11 and a half years later, not any closer to being an army nurse but still getting up and doing more before 9 a.m. than most people do all day, and I did not regret any of it.

Instead, I loved it. I loved the thrill of soldiering. It is about discipline, the brotherhood (and sisterhood), a sense of purpose and feeling like you are a part of something bigger than yourself. I loved the thrill of commanding soldiers, having them marching down and leading them in the cadence. I was in love with the chants: "Left, left-right, left." I think camouflage is in my blood. It grew on me. I loved going out into the field. I had fun sleeping outdoors—I could sleep in the winter or in the summer, if it wasn't raining, even when we weren't training. Yes, I am the epitome of Sergeant Major Wilson, and I am proud of it.

The lab training was something else. I would not say that if I learned goat lab, I mastered it. It was the part where we dissected goats. They were shot in the leg and brought to us in the lab, after which it was our responsibility to keep that goat alive for 24 hours. We did everything we could to make that happen. We got to do a chest tube, we did a venous cut-down, we intubated it, we sutured and we did anything that was possible. Ask me the consequence, my goat would survive. This was one of the many things that gave me the electricity to go; the list was long. NBC training, helicopters, rappelling out of helicopters, air assault certification, expert field medical badge, and running up PT are a few of the things I love. I could go on and on.

A noteworthy comment made by a friend of mine is something I can never forget. She came to me and told me that I used to change when I put on my uniform. Such remarks can prove to be eye-opening for you. When you are in the force, it's evident that you have to have your boots shined to a point where they look like glass, your uniform starched and everything in your attire in order. But she meant something else when she said to me, "Tonya, do you realize that when you put your uniform on, you're a different person?" It felt like a knife in the stomach. It gave me a reason to sit down, ponder and come to an understanding of what she had said.

I came to the realization that she was right. When I put that uniform and my hat on, I dropped all the nonsense immediately; I was not plain. I had to be what it took to get the job done, and I did not like the thought of that. I was not like that. In fact, I was an evangelist in the church of God in Christ; I was a mother, and I used to coach softball for young kids. But when I put on that uniform, I would forget every role of mine and I would just mean business.

You Will Be an Army Nurse

Eleven and a half years later, the dream of being an army nurse was nowhere to be chased. I was back in Columbus, Ohio with my boys, who were a treat to watch. I liked being around my family and friends, but it was my boys who were the most delighted to have me with them. They meant no business with the military. They just demanded me with their innocence to leave the army, and so I did.

I was finally at home. What did it mean at that time for me? I felt like I did not fit in. I found out that all I was worth was eight dollars an hour, even though I'd gone to EMT school, could sling load a Humvee into anywhere and could set up a hospital and save a life. Even though I could jump out of helicopters, drive a tank 113, shoot my M16 sharpshooter and throw a grenade, it all did not match the criteria for anything at my home. Even though I could command a whole unit, in Columbus, Ohio, I was not qualified to do anything. Nobody seemed to care about those double eagles on both sides of that uniform, or any of those things I mentioned. You have to start all over.

My new life was not at all a piece of cake. I started evaluating job opportunities and putting in applications, but I eventually realized I wasn't able to do anything but nursing. Unfortunately, there was no vacancy in the nursing schools. I was having a hard time processing and analyzing my situation. They were not happy thoughts, I admit. How was I going to manage with three sons and the babysitting fees being more than my check?

Surviving in the civilian world was becoming difficult due to other reasons too. Being a female soldier is not looked upon as greatly as it is in the military. In fact, it's quite the opposite. You are often ridiculed and treated badly. The fact that I had left my children and risked my life in war, for people who did not even seem to recognize that and appreciate the effort, was demoralizing. All that we had sacrificed was in return for what? It was degrading and horrible. I cannot explain in words how sad it was that there was no structure in the civilian world. I felt like a fish out of water.

Even while being depressed, I kept trying. Finally, after some worrisome days, I went to apply for a job at Ohio Health. Ohio Health is a big medical entity here in Ohio and a great hospital with many opportunities for nurses. I was offered two positions and, given my circumstances and my hard work routine, I accepted both of them. Not forgetting how we do more before 9 a.m. than most people do all day, I accepted one position at the Home Care office, and the other at the hospital. I enjoyed the challenge of the job and found satisfaction in being able to help patients, but it was mainly because I needed the money for my sons.

I was not used to needing so much money. Back in the military, one doesn't pay for medical or for dinner; in fact, you don't pay much for your meals as you get a food allowance. There were many other incentives as well. You get a housing allowance, hazardous pay and a gym membership; and if you live in base housing, you don't even pay rent or utilities. It was like I was dropped into Columbus, Ohio, an area that I could not understand.

I wanted to move out and stay in Clarksville, but there was no way that I could pull my kids away from the family once more. They hadn't seen their cousins. They were finally so happy to be home, and I could not take it away from them. Furthermore, they missed their dad, and they should not have moved away from him. Having said that, living close to their dad did not mean that he became an active participant in their life, but that's another story for another book.

True North

Let me recall what I learned about true north. Do I follow grid north, magnetic north or true north? I was able to get into a wonderful church of God in Christ. Pastor Rogers and Faith Tabernacle felt like home. Ohio Health was also able to be very instrumental for me. The Home Care Agency was just starting, and although I applied and was hired as a home health aide at $8 an hour, Fran Baby, my CEO, had planned something else for me. She recognized potential in me and saw that I had more talent than what I had been currently doing. As a result, she hired me for the position of a scheduler. This meant more pay and better use of my skills. I got to work with the intake department and helped create and build many things within the Home Care Agency.

I also worked on the hospital floor as a PCA. I was happy with the job, and I kept true to being a workaholic. I was achieving my goal of doing more before 9 a.m., along with being able to take care of my boys. I was making money to meet the financial needs of my children.

Thank You

After all that I had been through, I learned to let go. I had learned a lot of skills and how to release emotions that were stored or blocked. I was finally able to move on from the pain and hurt that I had experienced. I was now able to forgive those who had done me wrong and focus on the future. In addition, I still knew in my head that I needed to complete nursing school for the future. We did not have the greatest VA hospital in Columbus back then, but we do now. So, things have gotten better altogether. Thus, when Isaiah was a junior in high school, I went back to school and finally became a nurse. Although I never made it as an army nurse, I went to Chamberlain School of Nursing, and I graduated in 2009 with an associate's degree, and in 2010 with a bachelor's degree. I was able to achieve this by working hard and never giving up.

Even when things were tough, I kept moving forward. Look at me now; I can honestly say that I love my job as a "nurse," and the fact that today, the grandkids in my life have coined the name "TanktheNurse."

Final Thoughts

The next time that you say thank you for your service, I would like you to consider a few things: male, female, disabled, healthy, served one year, served 30-plus years, went to war, did not go to war.

There was a huge sacrifice made by every soldier who enlisted. I really don't think that people know the statistics on the number of people that we lose, not only just in war and combat but on a daily basis: friendly fire, accidents, suicide and also illnesses that are a result of serving in the armed forces.

In 2020, it was less than 1%. We had over 329.5 million Americans, with 0.727 percent of them actively serving. We currently have a population of over 330 million, with even less actively serving. It's something like 0.5 percent.

So again, less than 1% choose to make sacrifices and actively serve and protect the other 99%. Every branch is struggling with recruitment and getting soldiers.

But again, when you say thank you for your service, just take a moment and think about the sacrifices that soldiers like me, and thousands of others, have made.

Always remember that freedom isn't free. It comes at a price. That's why we need to show our appreciation and thank those who are brave enough to serve. Thank you for your service! You have my utmost respect and gratitude.

Made in the USA
Middletown, DE
08 June 2023

32230610R00066